Black-footed Ferret

National Conservation Center

*Environmental Assessment
For the Proposed Acquisition
of a New Administrative Site*

Table of Contents

Chapter 5. Coordination and Environmental Review 18

Chapter 1.
Purpose of and Need for Action

Introduction and Background

The black-footed ferret is a small, nocturnal carnivore closely related to minks, weasels, and badgers. Originally, the black-footed ferret ranged from the Canadian plains to the intermountain west and perhaps as far south as Mexico, but today it is the most endangered mammal in the United States (USFWS 1988). As early as 1967, populations had been reduced to the point where the species was officially recognized as endangered. A major cause for the decline in black-footed ferrets is thought to be the 90-98 percent reduction of the range of prairie dogs. Black-footed ferrets cannot survive outside of prairie dog towns, relying almost exclusively on prairie dogs for food and use of their burrows for shelter. Despite protection under the Endangered Species Act when it was enacted in 1973, by 1979, the last known ferrets had died and the species was declared extinct (USFWS 1988).

In 1981, a population of black-footed ferrets was discovered near Meeteetse, Wyoming, and the study and recovery of the species began again. Unfortunately, by 1985 canine distemper and sylvatic plague had a severe combined effect on the Meeteetse population and the remaining 18 ferrets of this population were brought into captivity (USFWS 1988). In 1987, a captive breeding program was initiated at the Wyoming Game and Fish Department's Sybille Wildlife Research Center near Wheatland, Wyoming in cooperation with the U.S. Fish and Wildlife Service. A year later, the Service revised and published a recovery plan for the black-footed ferret. The American Zoo and Aquarium Association also initiated a Species Survival Plan (SSP) and ferrets were sent to several zoos to create additional breeding populations. The SSP is considered the essential core of the endangered ferret population.

Today, over 50 percent of the captive-bred SSP black-footed ferrets come from the Sybille facility, which was renamed the National Black-Footed Ferret Conservation Center (FCC) after the Service assumed responsibility for managing the site in 1996. Several zoo breeding programs continue to contribute to the ferret population, as well as field breeding projects started in 1996. As of July 1999, through reintroductions in Montana, South Dakota, and Arizona, the number of ferrets in the wild (200) is larger than the last wild population at Meeteetse, Wyoming (130) (M. Lockhart, *pers. comm.*). This success is due in part to advances in breeding and preconditioning techniques which have increased survival rates of released ferrets. Continued development of these techniques, and expansion of the FCC to accommodate greater outdoor breeding and preconditioning, is critical to the black-footed ferret recovery program.

Proposed Action

The Service proposes to purchase a 40-acre parcel to be used as a new administrative site for the National Black-footed Ferret Conservation Center. The Ferret Conservation Center (FCC) is currently located at the Wyoming Game and Fish Department's Sybille Wildlife Research Center near Wheatland, Wyoming. The new site is located in Larimer County, Colorado (Figure 1), T. 10 N., R. 68 W., 6th P.M. Section 1: NW¼ SE¼ (Figure 2). The 40-acre parcel is part of the Meadow Springs Ranch, a 25,680-acre parcel owned by the City of Fort Collins.

Following the purchase of this property, the Service would construct several buildings for staff, maintenance, breeding, quarantine, and administration as well as 50-100 outdoor pens for breeding and preconditioning of ferrets. An access road approximately one-half mile in length also would be constructed to the site. The construction of the facility would be conducted in phases as funding becomes available.

Purpose of the Proposed Action

The purpose of the proposed action is to expand both the number and quality of ferrets produced in captivity. Since over half of the world's captive black-footed ferrets are at the FCC, these changes must occur primarily at this facility. The proposed new site for the FCC also will increase public access and awareness of the black-footed ferret and other endangered species recovery programs.

Need for the Proposed Action

The new ferret facility is needed for several reasons. Ferret production from zoos may decrease in the future, thus increasing the need for the FCC to sustain ferret production levels necessary to support reintroduction programs. The current facility at the Sybille Wildlife Research Center has no quarantine facility for infected ferrets, no expansion potential for pen breeding and preconditioning and the facility is currently located in a floodplain which could lead to catastrophic loss of the FCC. The remote location of the FCC also limits public access and awareness of the program.

Project Study Area

The proposed administrative site is located in Larimer County, Colorado approximately 22 miles north of Fort Collins and one-half mile east of Interstate 25. The 40-acre parcel is currently part of the Meadow Springs Ranch which is owned by the City of Fort Collins (Figure 3). The ranch includes 25,680 acres of gently rolling short-grass prairie ranging in elevation from 5,560-6,350 feet. Currently, the ranch is used by the City of Fort Collins for wastewater treatment; however, most of the activity takes place west of the proposed acquisition site and would not affect the property.

Decisions to be Made

Based on the analysis provided in this Environmental Assessment, the Regional Director of the U.S. Fish and Wildlife Service, Region 6-Mountain Prairie Region, will make three decisions:
1. Determine whether the Service should purchase a new site for the FCC facility. If yes,
2. Select an alternative for the acquisition of land for the new facility, and
3. Determine whether the selected alternative will have a significant impact upon the quality of the human environment. This decision is required by the National Environmental Policy Act (NEPA) of 1969. If the quality of the human environment is not significantly affected, a Finding of No Significant Impact will be signed and will be made available to the public. If the alternative is determined to have a significant impact, then an Environmental Impact Statement will be prepared to further address those impacts.

Issues Identified and Selected for Analysis

A press release describing the proposed acquisition and announcing a public scoping meeting was sent to six newspapers in the project area in October 1999. Congressional delegates for Colorado were also notified of the meeting. Eight people attended the public scoping meeting held in Fort Collins on October 27, 1999. No comments or issues were raised by the public at this meeting or during the subsequent comment period.

Biological Issues

The future of the black-footed ferret recovery program depends on the expanded production of ferrets and their successful reintroduction into the wild. Key components of this program include:
- the ability to maximize the production of ferrets and post-release survival through breeding and preconditioning in outdoor pens.
- the ability to protect black-footed ferrets from disease.
- raising public awareness and support of prairie conservation and associated effects on black-footed ferret and other endangered species programs.

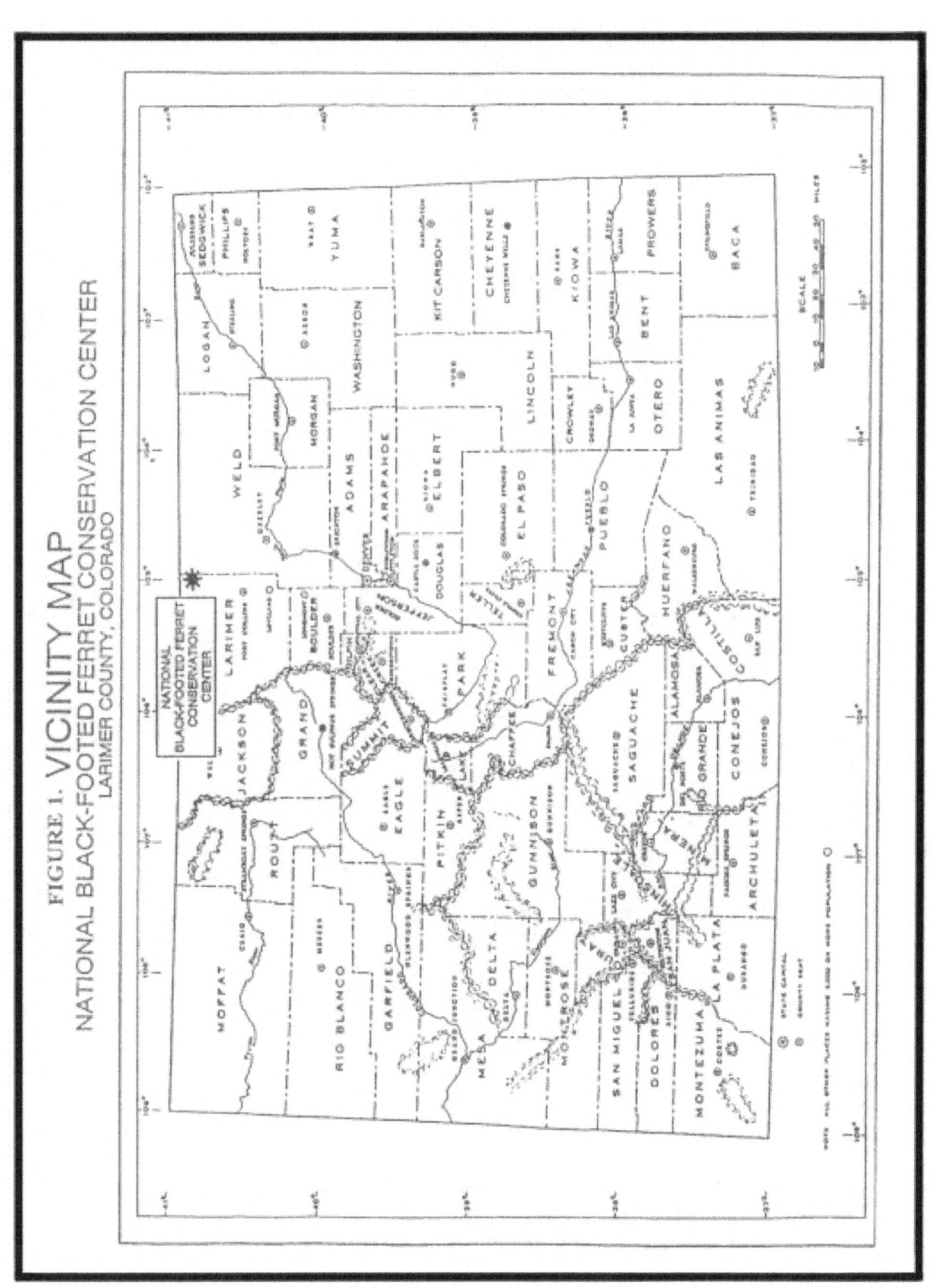

FIGURE 1. VICINITY MAP

NATIONAL BLACK-FOOTED FERRET CONSERVATION CENTER

LARIMER COUNTY, COLORADO

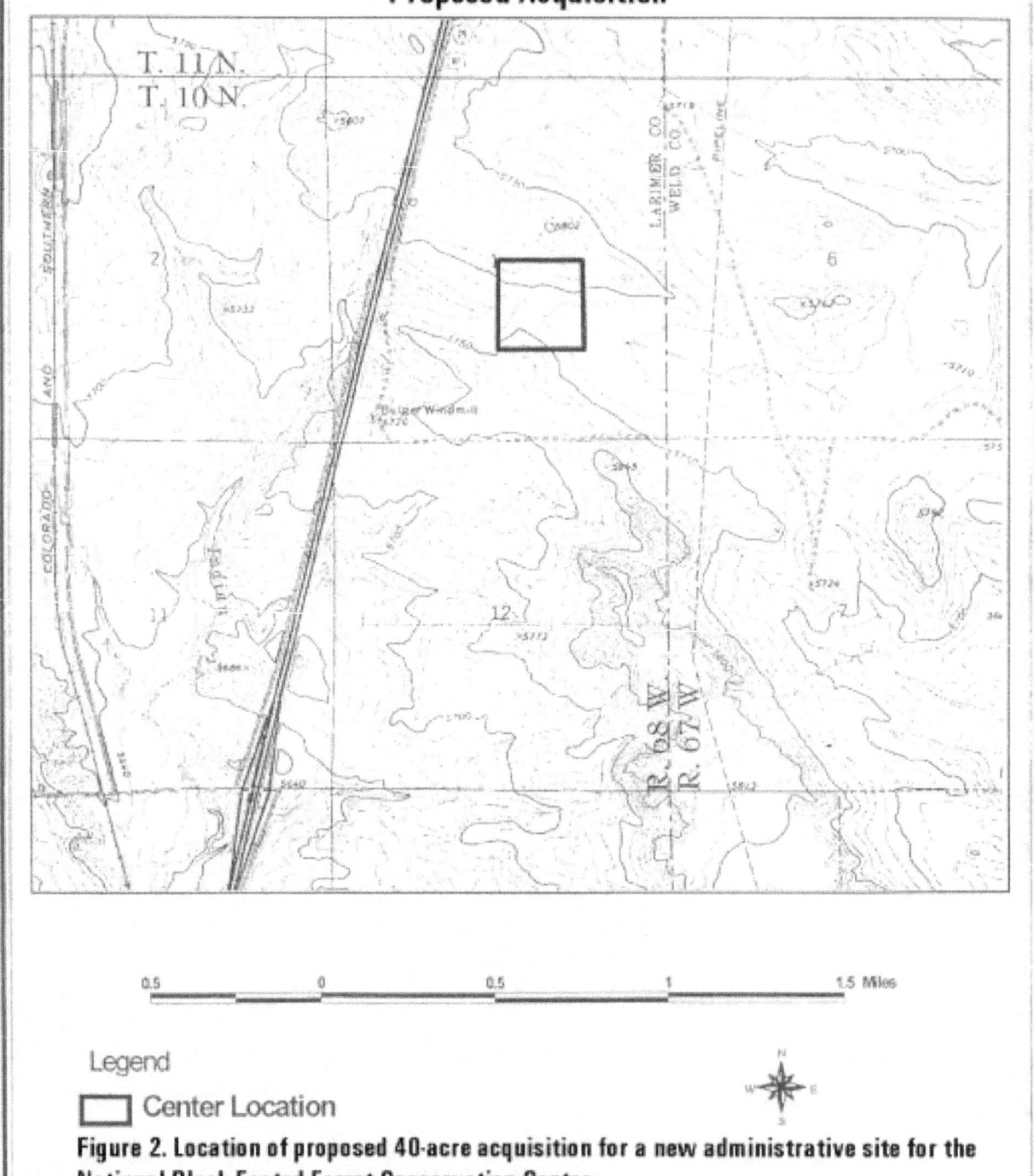

Figure 2. Location of proposed 40-acre acquisition for a new administrative site for the National Black-Footed Ferret Conservation Center.

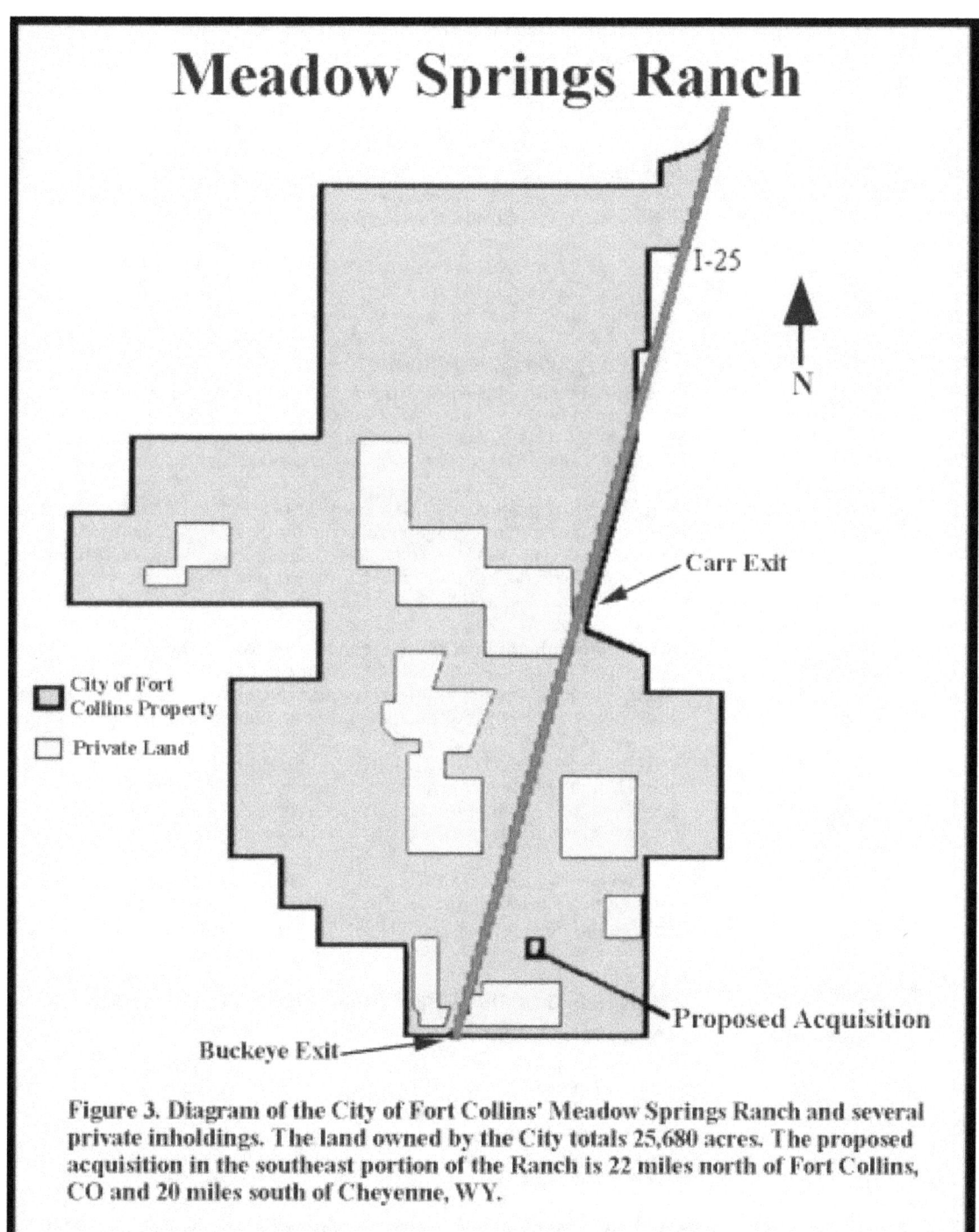

Meadow Springs Ranch

I-25

N

Carr Exit

City of Fort
Collins Property

Private Land

Proposed Acquisition

Buckeye Exit

Figure 3. Diagram of the City of Fort Collins' Meadow Springs Ranch and several private inholdings. The land owned by the City totals 25,680 acres. The proposed acquisition in the southeast portion of the Ranch is 22 miles north of Fort Collins, CO and 20 miles south of Cheyenne, WY.

Issues Identified but not Selected for Analysis

The following concern was noted by the Service, however, since the proposed action will have little or no impact on this concern, this topic was not evaluated further in the EA.

• The City of Fort Collins currently leases portions of the Meadow Springs Ranch to the Natural Fort Grazing Association for cattle grazing. If the Service purchases the proposed parcel for a new ferret facility, grazing may no longer be permitted within the 40-acre site.

Based on current grazing practices on the Ranch, the purchase of 40 acres by the Service would have little or no effect on the number of cows permitted under the lease (S. Comstock, *pers comm*).

Related Actions and Activities

Additional captive breeding sites under the Species Survival Plan for the black-footed ferret include the Phoenix Zoo (AZ), Louisville Zoo (KY), the National Zoo (VA), Cheyenne Mountain Zoo (CO), and the Toronto Zoo (Canada). Collectively, these zoos produced 230 kits in 1999.

Field breeding projects include a two year old project in Arizona where the first successful breeding and subsequent release of ferrets from an on-site facility occurred in 1998. Field breeding pens were also constructed or started in Colorado, Montana, and New Mexico in 1998. Eighteen percent of the kits produced in 1999 were born at field breeding facilities.

Reintroduction of black-footed ferrets has involved the states of Wyoming, Montana, South Dakota, Arizona, Colorado, and Utah. Shirley Basin, Wyoming was the first ferret reintroduction site which was initiated in 1991; but in 1994, reintroduction efforts in Shirley Basin were suspended due to an outbreak of plague. Sites in Montana, South Dakota, Arizona, and Utah are currently being used for reintroduction. The release site in South Dakota has been particularly successful with high production and survivorship of kits in the wild. No release sites are planned for north-central Colorado in conjunction with the proposed acquisition.

The Service is currently working with 31 groups to return ferrets to the wild. Agencies and organizations involved in the recovery effort include Federal and State agencies, tribal groups, and private, nonprofit organizations and zoos.

Purpose and Goals of the National Black-footed Ferret Conservation Center

The primary purposes of the FCC are 1) to produce ferrets for reintroduction, reestablish wild populations of black-footed ferrets in order to promote recovery of the species to the point where protection under the Endangered Species Act is no longer required; and 2) promote environmental education on ferrets, prairie dog communities, and prairie environments.

The purchase of the 40-acre parcel and relocation of the FCC would be consistent with the following relevant management plan:

1. The Black-footed Ferret Recovery Plan (USFWS 1988)

The Habitat Protection and Land Acquisition Process

Once the project is approved, the tract will be purchased from the City of Fort Collins using Service Construction Funds appropriated by Congress. The authority for the acquisition of 40 acres as a new administrative site is the Endangered Species Act of 1973.

Refuge Revenue Sharing Act

Under provisions of the Refuge Revenue Sharing Act (Public Law 95-469), the Service annually reimburses counties to offset revenue lost as a result of acquisition of property. This Law states that the Secretary of the Interior (Secretary) shall pay to each county in which any area acquired in fee title is situated, the greater of the following amounts:

1. An amount equal to the product of 75 cents multiplied by the total acreage of that portion of the fee area which is located within such county.
2. An amount equal to 3/4 of 1 percent of the fair market value, as determined by the Secretary, for that portion of the fee area which is located within such county.
3. An amount equal to 25 percent of the net receipts collected by the Secretary in connection with the operation and management of such fee area during such fiscal year. However, if a fee area is located in two or more counties, the amount for each county shall be apportioned in relationship to the acreage in that county.

The Refuge Revenue Sharing Act also requires that Service lands be reappraised every five years to ensure that payments to local governments remain equitable. Payments under this Act would be made only on lands that the Service acquires in fee title.

Chapter 2.
Alternatives, including the Preferred Action

Chapter 2 describes two alternatives: a No Action alternative and the Preferred Alternative to acquire 40 acres from the City of Fort Collins as a new site for the National Black-footed Ferret Conservation Center.

Alternative A. No Action.

Under the No Action alternative, the Service would not buy the 40-acre parcel from the City of Fort Collins and the National Black-footed Ferret Conservation Center would not be relocated to Colorado. If the parcel was not purchased, the National Black-footed Ferret Conservation Center would either remain at its current location at the Sybille Wildlife Research Center or be moved to another location. Other sites considered by the Service, within the historical range of the black-footed ferret, were less desirable due to weather extremes, high transportation costs, limited public access, and/or significant distances from veterinary and research facilities.

Alternative B. Acquisition of 40 acres on the City of Fort Collins' Meadow Springs Ranch as a new location for the National Black-footed Ferret Conservation Center (Preferred Alternative).

Under Alternative B, the Service would purchase a 40-acre parcel from the City of Fort Collins (Figure 2). The site would provide a new location for the National Black-footed Ferret Conservation Center. Following the purchase of this property, the Service would construct several buildings for staff, maintenance, breeding, quarantine, and administration as well as 50-100 outdoor pens for breeding and preconditioning of ferrets. An access road approximately one-half mile in length also would be constructed to the site. Construction of the facility would be conducted in phases as funding becomes available.

Chapter 3.
Affected Environment

This chapter describes the existing biological, social, economic, and cultural resources that would most likely be affected by this acquisition.

Biological Environment

The proposed 40-acre acquisition is located in north-central Colorado in the Great Plains-Palouse Dry Steppe ecoregional province (Bailey 1995). This is a semiarid region with an average rainfall of 15 inches per year, primarily from summer thunderstorms and winter snow (RBD Inc. and Camp, Dresser and McKee Inc. 1994). The average annual temperature is 45° F, with cold winters and hot summers (Bailey 1995).

The 40-acre parcel is situated over a relatively flat area, with elevations ranging from 5,740 to 5,760 feet (Figure 2). Ridges lie to the north and south of the parcel and ephemeral stream drainages to the east and west. Soils on the parcel are well-drained loams and fine, sandy loams of the Altvan-Larimer-Stoneham soil association. No wetlands exist on the parcel. Vegetation on the tract is typical native short-grass prairie which is characterized by blue grama, buffalo grass, and western wheatgrass, as well as a variety of forbs.

The proposed acquisition is part of the Meadow Springs Ranch, a 25,680-acre parcel owned by the City of Fort Collins for wastewater treatment. The Ranch has a gently rolling topography ranging in elevation from 5,560-6,350 feet. Vegetation on the Ranch is native short-grass prairie with common species including blue grama, buffalo grass, western wheatgrass, and fringed sage. Wildlife surveys have found 13 species of mammals on the Ranch; thirteen-lined ground squirrels, desert cottontails, and pronghorns are especially common. One hundred species of birds also have been recorded, including abundant numbers of horned larks, McCown's longspurs, and western meadowlarks (RBD Inc. and Camp, Dresser and McKee Inc. 1994).

Ferruginous hawks, burrowing owls, and loggerhead shrikes are U.S. Fish and Wildlife Service species of concern that have been known to nest on the Ranch, although not on the proposed acquisition (USFWS 1995, RBD Inc. and Camp, Dresser and McKee Inc. 1994). In 1992, the mountain plover, now a species proposed for listing under the Endangered Species Act, nested in the northwest corner of the section approximately one-half mile from the proposed acquisition. To the southeast of the proposed acquisition is a black-tailed prairie dog town. Also, a record exists of a swift fox den on the Ranch. The black-tailed prairie dog and swift fox are currently candidates for listing under the Endangered Species Act.

Social and Economic Considerations

The Meadow Springs Ranch, on which the proposed acquisition is located, is owned and operated by the City of Fort Collins as a site for disposal of biosolids from the City's wastewater treatment facilities. Several private inholdings exist on the Ranch, and the Ranch is bordered by private lands.

The 40-acre parcel is located 22 miles north of Fort Collins, Colorado, population 115,000, and 20 miles south of Cheyenne, Wyoming which is the capitol of Wyoming and has a population of 53,000.

Agricultural Resources

The Ranch has a history of cattle grazing, mining, and limited farming. Cattle grazing is still permitted on portions of the Ranch, including the proposed 40-acre acquisition. The 40-acre parcel, however, has never been plowed for farming.

Landownership

The 40-acre parcel is currently owned by the City of Fort Collins. No new or additional zoning or land-use regulations would be created by the Service within the proposed acquisition or for neighboring landowners.

Property Tax

The City of Fort Collins does not currently pay taxes on the proposed acquisition. Upon acquisition of the 40-acre parcel by the Service, Larimer County will receive payment-in-lieu-of-taxes from the Service under the Refuge Revenue Sharing Act (see Chapter 1). This payment is currently estimated to be $240 annually.

Public Use and Wildlife-Dependent Activities

The City of Fort Collins did discuss limited public use on the Meadow Springs Ranch in the overall design of their Master Plan; however, no public use occurs on the proposed acquisition currently. Once the Service purchases the 40-acre parcel and visitor facilities at the National Black-footed Ferret Conservation Center are complete, the site will be open to public access.

Cultural Resources

Archaeological and historical resources within any fee title lands receive protection under Federal laws mandating the management and protection of cultural resources. These laws included, but are not limited to, the Archaeological Resources Protection Act, the Archaeological and Historic Preservation Act, the Native American Graves Protection and Repatriation Act, Native American Religion Freedom Act, and the National Historic Preservation Act.

The Service has met with the Regional Archaeologist to be certain that the action of purchasing the proposed acquisition and the subsequent construction of the new National Black-footed Ferret Conservation Center complies with Section 106 of the National Historic Preservation Act (NHPA) of 1966, as amended. The Service will also make certain that any future projects, programs or activities that will result in changes to the character of, or will potentially adversely affect, any historic cultural resources or archaeological site are also in compliance with the NHPA.

Contaminants and Hazardous Wastes

A preliminary Level I survey of the proposed acquisition determined that no contaminants exist on the parcel that would pose a threat to wildlife and people or would be a liability to the Service.

Chapter 4.
Environmental Consequences

This section assesses the environmental impacts expected to occur from the implementation of Alternatives A or B as described in Chapter 2. Environmental impacts are analyzed by issues for each alternative and appear in the same order as presented in Chapter 1.

Effects on the Biological Environment
Black-footed Ferret Breeding and Reintroduction

Alternative A (No Action): Under the No Action Alternative, the Service would not purchase 40 acres from the City of Fort Collins as a new site for the National Black-footed Ferret Conservation Center. Therefore, no improvements would be associated with the new facility or an increase in the number of outdoor pens for ferret breeding and preconditioning. The consequence of choosing the No Action alternative would be slower progress in reaching the goals of the black-footed ferret recovery program.

If the new 40-acre site is not purchased, the 50-100 outdoor pens planned for the new facility site would not be constructed. The ferret recovery program would continue to use the 18 outdoor pens at the Sybille facility and 6 pens at Warren Air Force Base. The area of these pens is considered too small to meet the demands of the program, and it would not be possible to expand the outdoor pen area or improve their quality due to space limitations.

Although the ferret recovery program has made significant advances since its creation in 1987, several limiting factors in the current facility were identified during a site planning visit. The current breeding facility is not large enough to allow efficient management and cleaning of the ferret cages. The surgery room does not have space for ferret recovery or adequate storage space for supplies and equipment. Space does not exist to expand the hamster colony, an important whole food source for ferrets. The storage and maintenance facilities for equipment to run the facility are limited and the residence for Service personnel is in poor condition. Given that zoo breeding programs may be scaled back over the next several years, and the FCC already produces over 50 percent of program ferrets, management limitations on the FCC greatly reduce the overall efficiency and capabilities of the ferret recovery program.

The current prairie dog quarantine facility, to assure that infectious diseases are not passed to ferrets, is outdoors and thus is limited to use in summer months. If the Service does not create a new site for the FCC, opportunities to precondition ferrets with prairie dogs, which ultimately increases reintroduced ferrets' survival rates, will continue to be restricted.

The Sybille facility is 47 miles from Laramie, Wyoming, the nearest major city. This remote location, in combination with bad weather which often closes the road to the site, limits public access to the site and public awareness of the ferret recovery program. If the FCC remains in its present location, opportunities for public education and increased support necessary for the success of the recovery program will be lost.

If the Service selects the No Action alternative, the new site for the FCC would not be purchased and progress of the recovery program would not be enhanced. The resulting slower progress may have several negative consequences. The length of time to meet the ultimate goal of 10 wild, breeding populations may be greater which ultimately increases the total cost of black-footed ferret recovery. Delays in reaching the program goals may erode the support base from agencies and organizations outside of the Service. In addition, slower progress means that the ferret population would spend more time in captivity which will ultimately reduce overall species fitness. By extending captivity, genetic diversity is reduced, innate or 'wild' behaviors may be lost and natural selection no longer acts on the species (Biggins *et al.* 1998).

Alternative B (Purchase of a 40-acre parcel—Preferred Alternative):

Under this Alternative the Service would purchase a 40-acre parcel from the City of Fort Collins as a new administrative site for the National Black-footed Ferret Conservation Center. The short-grass prairie habitat of the new site more closely resembles black-footed ferret habitat than habitat at the current facility. More significantly, the new site would provide room to expand the FCC's outdoor pen rearing capabilities from 18 pens to 50-100 pens. The new pens would have substantial security measures to prevent ferret escape.

The additional pen rearing capability that will become possible through the purchase of land for the new site has several advantages to the black-footed ferret recovery program. The number of ferret kits that can be produced in outdoor pens is higher than traditional cage rearing (M. Lockhart, *pers. comm.*). Pen rearing also has been shown to dramatically increase the survival rates of ferrets reintroduced to the wild. After one month, survival was 2.7 times higher for pen reared ferrets than cage reared animals and after nine months, survival of pen reared ferrets was 10 times higher (Biggins *et al.* 1998). In fact, survival rates of reintroduced ferrets that were reared were similar to survival rates for the last known wild population of ferrets near Meeteetse, Wyoming.

Existing data suggest that the length of time spent in outdoor pens may be directly related to survival rates. Predation is the main cause of mortality of reintroduced ferrets, and it is thought that pen rearing improves survivorship by enabling ferrets to improve predator avoidance skills. Additional benefits of pen rearing include less contact and habituation with humans, increased hunting skills, and increased physical condition (Biggins *et al.* 1998).

Purchasing the 40-acre parcel and creating a new FCC facility will also benefit the recovery of the black-footed ferret through improvements in efficiency and management quality. Changes in the breeding center, surgery facilities and storage capacity and organization will make the overall care and breeding of the ferrets more efficient and effective. In addition, space will be available to improve the hamster colony, thus increasing the quality of the ferret diet.

Acquisition of the 40-acre parcel for a new FCC facility will improve the Service's ability to protect ferrets from disease. The new facility will improve and expand both quarantine facilities for prairie dogs and the ferret isolation center to prevent the spread of disease between ferrets. Furthermore, outdoor pen rearing is thought to increase ferrets' resistence to soil pathogens, which may improve survival rates upon reintroduction (Biggins *et al.* 1998).

The location of the proposed acquisition also will increase public awareness of the ferret recovery program through improved access to the FCC. The new site will be only 22 miles north of Fort Collins, Colorado (pop. 115,000) and approximately 20 miles south of Cheyenne, Wyoming (pop. 53,000). In addition, the facility will be one-half mile east of Interstate 25, a major north-south travel route. The FCC will be visible from the Interstate and readily accessible via a nearby exit. The new facility will have a public contact area and interpretive displays. Increased public access is essential to achieving recovery objectives and will be enhanced greatly at the new site.

The proposed acquisition has the potential to substantially improve ferret reintroduction capabilities (Biggins *et al.* 1998). Such improvements ultimately will help the Service meet species recovery goals, currently defined as 10 populations of wild ferrets with at least 30 breeding adults by the year 2010, in a more timely and cost efficient manner (USFWS 1988).

Unavoidable Adverse Impacts

The selection of Alternative B may result in unavoidable adverse impacts. Although the purchase of the 40-acre parcel would not have adverse impacts, the subsequent construction and establishment of the facility will result in the loss of about 10 acres of native, short-grass prairie habitat. Plans will be developed by the Service to avoid or minimize any potential effects of this action on species listed under the Endangered Species Act. The selection of the No Action alternative also may have adverse impacts on the ferret recovery program by delaying or preventing improvements needed to meet species recovery goals.

Irreversible and Irretrievable Commitments of Resources

Alternative A, the No Action alternative, would not result in any irreversible or irretrievable commitments of resources. However, other solutions for meeting the needs of the ferret recovery program would need to be developed, which could result in a commitment of resources greater than those expected with Alternative B. Under Alternative B, purchase of the 40-acre parcel would require an irreversible and irretrievable commitment of resources to purchase the property. Once the site is purchased, further commitment of resources would occur to construct the new National Black-footed Ferret Conservation Center as well as future expenditures to operate the facility.

Short-term Uses Versus Long-term Productivity

Alternative B, to purchase 40 acres as a new site for the National Black-footed Ferret Conservation Center (FCC), will enhance both short-term and long-term productivity. In the short-term, the new administrative site will enable the FCC to increase the production and quality of captive-bred ferrets for reintroduction to the wild. Improved public access associated with the new site also will increase public awareness of the black-footed ferret and endangered species in general. This will ultimately help the black-footed ferret recovery program meet established goals set for 2010. Since the site is located near two large cities and is easily accessible via Interstate 25, it could be used for other endangered species programs, public outreach, or as a research facility, if in the future, the site is no longer needed for the ferret program.

Cumulative Impacts

The purchase of the 40-acre parcel for a new administrative site for the National Black-footed Ferret Conservation Center would have beneficial, long-term, cumulative effects. The improvements in the facility, made possible through the new site, will further recovery of the black-footed ferret and are considered essential to successfully returning ferrets to the wild. Furthermore, the increased public access to the new facility can be expected to improve public awareness and support for endangered species recovery in general, thus providing benefits to future recovery efforts for other species.

Chapter 5.
Coordination and Environmental Review

Agency Coordination

The screening process to find a new site for the National Black-footed Ferret Conservation Center began in 1998. The Service reviewed potential locations in six western states in coordination with the Black-footed Ferret Recovery Implementation Team. The Black-footed Ferret Recovery Implementation Team is comprised of Federal and State government agencies, Native American tribes, zoos, and conservation organizations. Once Fort Collins, Colorado was identified as a preferred location, the Service made preliminary inquiries into land availability. Subsequent discussions with the Water Utilities Office of the City of Fort Collins led to the proposed acquisition of 40 acres addressed in this Environmental Assessment.

National Environmental Policy Act

As a Federal agency, the U.S. Fish and Wildlife Service must comply with provisions of the National Environmental Policy Act (NEPA). An Environmental Assessment is required under NEPA to evaluate reasonable alternatives that will meet stated objectives and to assess the possible impacts to the human environment. The Environmental Assessment serves as the basis for determining whether implementation of the proposed action would constitute a major Federal action significantly affecting the quality of the human environment. The Environmental Assessment also facilitates the involvement of government agencies and the public in the decision making process.

Other Federal Laws, Regulations, and Executive Orders

In undertaking the proposed action, the Service would comply with a number of Federal laws, executive orders, and legislative act, including: Floodplain Management (Executive Order 11988); Intergovernmental Review of Federal Programs (Executive Order 12372); Protection of Historical, Archaeological, and Scientific Properties (Executive Order 11593); Protection of Wetlands (Executive Order 11990); Endangered Species Act of 1973, as amended; Uniform Relocation Assistance and Real Property Acquisition Policy Act of 1970, as amended; National Historic Preservation Act of 1966, as amended.

Distribution and Availability

Copies of this Environmental Assessment were sent to Federal, State, and City agencies as well as interested individuals. Additional copies of this document are available at U.S. Fish and Wildlife Service Office, 134 Union Blvd., Suite 350, Lakewood, Colorado 80228 (tel. 303-236-8145, ext. 658).

List of Preparers and Reviewers
Author:
Vanessa Hill, Biological Technician, Land Acquisition and Refuge Planning, Division of Realty, Refuges and Wildlife, Bismarck, ND

Reviewers:
Susan Baker, Acting Assistant Regional Director, Ecological Services, Lakewood, CO

Jill Parker, Chief, Endangered Species, Lakewood, CO

Larry Shanks, Acting GARD, Southern Ecosystems, Lakewood, CO

Carol Taylor, Supervisor Fishery Resources/Ecological Services, Southern Ecosystems, Lakewood, CO

Susan Linner, Supervisor Ecological Services, Northern Ecosystems, Lakewood, CO

Harvey Wittmier, Chief, Division of Realty, Refuges and Wildlife, Lakewood, CO

John Esperance, Fish and Wildlife Biologist, Land Acquisition and Refuge Planning, Division of Realty, Refuges and Wildlife, Lakewood, CO

Pete Gober, Field Supervisor, Ecological Services, Pierre, SD

Mike Lockhart, Fish and Wildlife Biologist, National Black-footed Ferret Conservation Center, Laramie, WY

Barbara Shupe, Writer/Editor, Land Acquisition and Refuge Planning, Division of Realty, Refuges and Wildlife, Lakewood, CO

Acknowledgments:
Jaymee Fojtik, Cartographer, Land Acquisition and Refuge Planning, Division of Realty, Refuges and Wildlife, Lakewood, CO

Jim Sinclair, Senior Appraiser, Division of Realty, Refuges and Wildlife, Lakewood, CO

References

Bailey, R.G. 1995. Description of Ecoregions of the United States. U.S. Forest Service Miscellaneous publication no. 1391. Washington, D.C. http://www.fs.fed.us/colormap/ecoreg1_home.html

Biggins, DE, Godbey, JL, Hanebury, LR, Luce, B, Marinari, PE, Matchett, MR and A Vargas. 1998. The effect of rearing methods on survival of reintroduced black-footed ferrets. J of Wildl Manage 62(2):643-653.

Comstock, S., Water Reclamation Department Manager, Water Utilities Office of the City of Fort Collins, Phone Interview, February 2000.

Lockhart, M., Fish and Wildlife Biologist, Black-footed Ferret Recovery Program. Personal communication during site visit, February 2000.

RBD, and Camp, Dresser and McKee. 1994. Master plan for biosolids and water treatment plant residuals Volume 1. Prepared for: City of Fort Collins, Fort Collins, CO.

USFWS. 1988. Black-footed ferret recovery plan. U.S. Fish and Wildlife Service, Denver, CO 154pp.

USFWS. 1995. Migratory nongame birds of management concern in the United States: the 1995 list. Office of Migratory Bird Management, Washington D.C.

Appendix A.
Endangered, Threatened, and Candidate Species

Listed Species*

black-footed ferret(E)	*Mustela nigripes*
Eskimo curlew (E)	*Numenius borealis*
whooping crane (E)	*Grus americana*
bald eagle (T)	*Haliaeetus leucocephalus*
greenback cutthroat trout (T)	*Oncorhynchus clarki stomias*
Mexican spotted owl (T)	*Strix occidentalis lucida*
pallid sturgeon (T)	*Scaphirhynchus albus*
Preble's meadow jumping mouse (T)	*Zapus hudsonius preblei*
Ute ladies'-tresses (T)	*Spiranthes diluvialis*

Proposed species

Canada lynx (T)	*Lynx canadensis*
Colorado butterfly plant (T)	*Gaura neomexicana* ssp. *coloradensis*
mountain plover (T)	*Charadrius montanus*

Candidate species

black-tailed prairie dog	*Cynomys ludovicianus*
boreal toad	*Bufo boreas boreas*
swift fox	*Vulpes velox*

* The species listed here are those reported in the vicinity or surrounding area (Larimer County), not necessarily in the proposed project area.

Appendix B.
Distribution List for the Environmental Assessment

Federal Officials

P   Senator Wayne Allard
P   Senator Ben Nighthorse Campbell
P   Representative Bob Schaffer

Federal Agencies

P   USDA, Natural Resources Conservation Service
P   USDA, Farm Services Agency
P   US Fish and Wildlife Service
     Southern Ecosystems, Region 6, Lakewood, CO
     Northern Ecosystems, Region 6, Lakewood, CO
     Ecological Services, Region 6, Lakewood, CO
     Ecological Services-South Dakota, Pierre, SD

State Government

P   Colorado Division of Wildlife
P   Colorado State Clearinghouse
P   Wyoming Game and Fish Department

City of Fort Collins

P   Mayor of Fort Collins
P   Water Utilities Office

Individuals and Organizations

P   Natural Fort Grazing Association
P   Individuals (7)

Appendix C.
List of Common and Scientific Names Used in the Text

Plants

blue grama	*Bouteloua gracilis*
buffalo grass	*Buchloe dactyloides*
western wheatgrass	*Pascopyrum smithii*
fringed sage	*Artemesia frigida*

Wildlife

black-footed ferret	*Mustela nigripes*
black-tailed prairie dog	*Cynomys ludovicianus*
desert cottontail	*Sylvilagus auduboni*
pronghorn	*Antilocapra americana*
swift fox	*Vulpes velox*
thirteen-lined ground squirrel	*Spermophilus tridecemlineatus*
burrowing owl	*Athene cuncularia*
ferruginous hawk	*Buteo regalis*
horned lark	*Eremophila alpestris*
loggerhead shrike	*Lanius ludovicianus*
mountain plover	*Charadrius montanus*
McCown's longspur	*Calcarius mccownii*
western meadowlark	*Sternella neglecta*

Disease

sylvatic plague	*Yersinia pestis*